From an old Cookbook TURKEY- DUCK - WILD GAME
by D Lan

From an old cookbook TURKEY DUCK WILD GAME

Table of Contents

1. Pre — 5
2. Standard Method of Roasting Turkey — 7
3. CHESTNUT STUFFING FOR TURKEY — 9
4. GAME HENS — 11
5. GAME HENS WITH WILD RICE STUFFING — 12
6. BROILED GAME HENS WITH DRESSING — 14
7. ROAST PHEASANT WITH CRANBERRIES — 16
8. ROAST TURKEY IN FOIL — 19
9. TURKEY BROILER WITH PECAN STUFF — 20
10. TURKEY WITH MUSHROOM DRESSING — 22
11. TURKEY HASH — 24
12. BARBECUED TURKEY BROILERS — 25
13. CURRIED TURKEY AMANDINE — 27
14. SPAGHETTI TURKEY CASSEROLE — 29
15. TURKEY GLACE — 30
16. OYSTER HAM STUFFING — 32
17. CORN-BREAD OYSTER STUFFING — 33
18. POLONAISE BREAD STUFFING — 34
19. CHICKEN-LIVER RICE STUFFING — 35
20. CORN BREAD STUFFING — 36
21. WHEAT PILAF STUFFING — 37
22. TURKEY DIVAN — 38
23. SQUABS WITH BLACK OLIVES — 39
24. Garnishes appropriate to CHICKEN (WHITE-MEAT BIRDS) TURKEY — 41
25. ROAST DUCK WITH ORANGE SAUCE — 42
26. ROAST DUCKLING PIQUANTE — 44

27. SWEET AND SOUR ROAST DUCK	46
28. PINEAPPLE DUCK (Chinese Duck)	48
29. PLANKED DUCKLING	49
30. DUCK IN CASSEROLE	51
31. DUCK WITH APPLE SAUERKRAUT STUFFING	53
32. BROILED DUCKLING	55
33. ROAST DUCK WITH ORANGE STUFFING	56
34. DUCKUNG BIGARADE	58
35. ROAST GOOSE WITH PRUNE STUFFING	60
36. ROAST GOOSE	62
37. POACHED GOOSE	64
38. Herbs and Garnishes appropriate to DUCK-GOOSE- SOUAB	66
39. WILD GAME	67
40. GAME BIRDS	68
41. ROAST WILD DUCK	70
42. ROAST WILD DUCK DELUXE	71
43. ROAST MALLARD DUCK	72
44. BREAST OF WILD DUCK-SAUCE BIGARADE	74
45. QUAIL	76
46. ROAST QUAIL	77
47. BREASTS OF PARTRIDGE OR PHEASANT	78
48. FRIED PHEASANT	80
49. GROUSE	81
50. GROUSE BAKED	82
51. BROILED PARTRIDGE	83
52. GROUSE IN CASSEROLE	84
53. WILD GOOSE	85
54. VENISON	86
55. VENISON ROAST	87

56. VENISON ROAST DELUXE	**89**
57. ROAST SADDLE OF VENISON	**91**
58. VENISON STEW	**94**
59. RABBIT	**95**
60. HASENPFEFFER	**96**
61. BRAISED RABBIT	**98**
62. FRIED RABBIT	**99**
63. RABBIT STEW	**100**
64. RABBIT FRICASSEE	**102**
65. Herbs and Garnishings	**104**
66. Acknowledgements	**105**

From an old cookbook TURKEY DUCK WILD GAME

1. Pre

TURKEY

As is it has been said chicken is for every Sunday as turkey is for Thanksgiving and other major occasions, holidays and since it is available all year round and is a great idea to accommodate many guests on a reasonable budget for any dinner, with leftovers including good to the last drop soup de turkey.

Variety:
Teen-agers weighing from 3 to 6 pounds are delicious broiled or fried-the larger of these lending themselves better to frying. When buying these, be sure to get a young bird-not just a small one.
Slightly older hens or toms may weigh in at anywhere between 7 and 20 pounds and the seniors of both sexes go up to 30 pounds. All of these are for roasting.

SQUABS

Squabs are young pigeons, the younger the better. They have dark, delicious rich meat and may be roasted, sautéed, broiled, or potted. As they are small birds, weighing about 1 lb. which is usually one squab per serving. These young pigeons are wonderful luncheon party fare.

DUCKS AND GEESE

5

These birds are kissing cousins of the chicken, but their flesh is darker and richer in wild flavor. The favorite cooking method is roasting, but they may also be braised or boiled. Baby ducklings can also be broiled. North American ducks and geese are rich in fat and additional fat rub or coating is not recommended before being cooked. Foreign chefs who may probably be accustomed to the European varieties, which are thinner and dryer.

Prepare for cooking as you would chicken and turkey. When roasting, do not cover the bird, any ways you don't even need to baste it for the bird to remain juicy. However, you may baste with fruit juice, wine or other. Prick the skin of a fat duck or any goose to let the fat which is just under the skin run out and naturally baste the bird. It is important also to keep remove excess the fat from the pan as it accumulates.

2. Standard Method of Roasting Turkey

Standard Method of Roasting Turkey

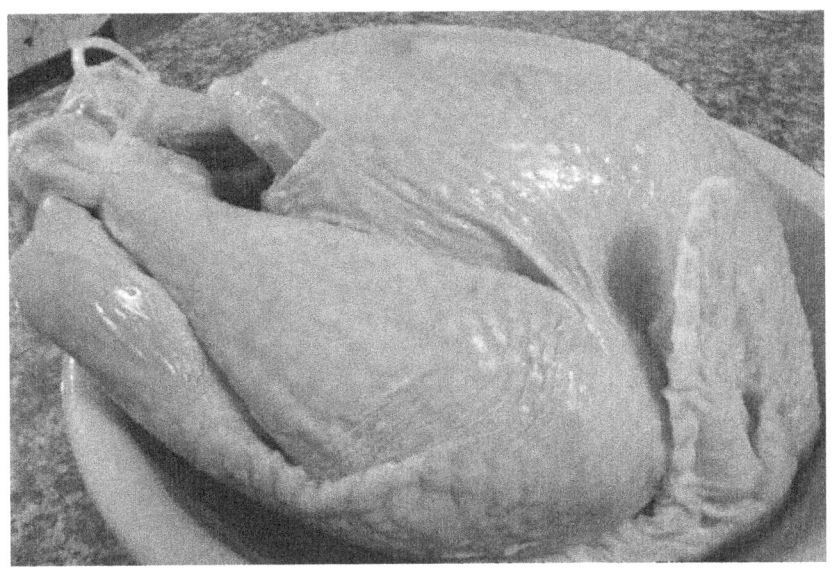

Preparation:

Wash the turkey, pat dry inside and out. singe, and remove any stray or small pinfeathers with tweezers. Cut a small V and remove the oil sac from the tail. Remove the neck if the butcher didn't. Allow 1 1/4 cups of stuffing per pound of turkey.
Completely fill the body of the turkey and neck cavity with stuffing. Fasten the openings by sewing shut with cord or using poultry pins or skewers whatever works best for you. Tuck and fold the wing tips back and down under in toward the body. The wings will help keep the bird from moving while cooking in the roast pan and on the platter. Bring the legs together and tie them together securely then with the same piece of cord tie to the tail not

too tight. Prepare the bird by rubbing soft butter or margarine all over the turkey roast in a preheated oven @325° for 3 to 4 hours for an 8 to 10 lb. bird and 4 to 5 hours for birds up to 14 lbs. and 5 to 7 hours for birds up to 20 lbs. Roast in open pan with no Water, basting occasionally with extra butter at first and then with drippings. If the turkey is becoming too brown, cover the bird with a piece of cheesecloth or use aluminum foil loosely fit to cover the top removable so you may baste the turkey so that it remains moist. Remove the covering for the last 15 to 30 minutes to allow the skin to become crispy and turn golden brown.

3. CHESTNUT STUFFING FOR TURKEY

CHESTNUT STUFFING FOR TURKEY

Ingredients:

For a 16-22 pound turkey:
3 (1 lb.) loaves day-old bread
I cup butter
3 cloves garlic crushed (optional)
3 cups Chopped celery and celery leaves
2 1/2 cups Chopped onion
2 pounds chestnuts boiled
3 tablespoons salad oil
6 tablespoons chopped parsley
1 tablespoon salt
1/2 teaspoon freshly ground pepper
2 tablespoons basil
1 tablespoon marjoram
1 teaspoon sage

Preparation:

Spread out the bread slices and let them stand at room temperature overnight. Remove crusts and pick bread apart into small flakes with your fingers. In a large skillet over medium heat melt 1/2 cup butter add the garlic to infuse the oil just cook 1 minute, then add the celery, onion and cook until lightly brown. Cool to lukewarm, empty contents of skillet over bread and mix thoroughly. Peel the chestnuts and chop coarsely. To remove shells and skin from chestnuts, make V-shaped cut in hat side of each nut, spread them out on pan or baking sheet and pour a little salad oil over them. Toss and turn them to coat with oil. Put pan in preheated oven @450° for 10 minutes. Remove from oven and cool. Shell and skin when cool add nuts to stuffing with parsley. Season with salt and pepper. Put the rest of the butter in the skillet and add the basil, marjoram and sage. Put butter and herbs over low heat for a minute to release and infuse the flavors also you can add the herb mixture to stuffing while tossing. The stuffing should be light, not packed or compressed, and is now ready to stuff into the turkey.

4. GAME HENS

GAME HENS

Ingredients:

6 Cornish game hens
1 teaspoon salt
1/2 teaspoon pepper
3 bouillon cubes
2 1/2 cups water
1/3 cup lemon iuice
Flour

Preparation:

Remove the giblets, rinse hens in cold water, dry, and place the bird in uncovered roasting pan on rack , breast side up. Salt and pepper them. Dissolve the bouillon cubes in water and add the lemon juice. Pour over the hens and roast in preheated oven 425° for 60 minutes or more until tender, basting frequently. Can be served garnished with orange slices topped with currant jelly to taste.
In a large saucepan over medium heat you can make gravy by simmering the giblets in water, add flour to the pan drippings and add the water in which the giblets were cooked. Add giblets if you like. Season to taste with salt and pepper.

Makes: 6 servings

5. GAME HENS WITH WILD RICE STUFFING

GAME HENS WITH WILD RICE STUFFING

Ingredients::

6 Cornish game hens
1 teaspoon salt
6 slices bacon
2 tablespoons butter

Stuffing:
1 cup wild rice
1/2 cup chopped onion
1/2 pound mushrooms sliced
1 1/2 cups diced or chopped cooked ham
6 tablespoons butter
1/2 teaspoon salt
1/2 teaspoon marjoram
1/2 teaspoon thyme

Preparation:
Stuffing: Wash and cook the rice according to directions on the package. Drain. In a large saucepan over medium heat sauté the onion, mushrooms and ham in the butter for 5 minutes. Mix with rice. Season with salt, marjoram and thyme. Makes about 3 1/2 cups of stuffing, which is enough for 6 game hens.

Season cavities or hens with salt. Stuff the birds with the stuffing then truss then. Lay 2 half-slices of bacon over each bird, you should add a little butter to the pan, and roast, uncovered, in preheated oven @350° for 90 minutes or until tender and browned, basting regularly with pan drippings.

Makes: 6 servings

6. BROILED GAME HENS WITH DRESSING

BROILED GAME HENS WITH DRESSING

Ingredients:

From an old cookbook TURKEY DUCK WILD GAME

8 Cornish game hens split
5 tablespoons butter
4 cups coarsely chopped celery
4 cups coarsely chopped mushrooms
5 teaspoons salt
V2 teaspoon rosemary
V2 teaspoon thyme
3/3 teaspoon pepper
1 cup coarsely chopped water chestnuts
1 cup flour

Preparation:
In a large skillet melt 1 tablespoon butter. Add celery, mushrooms, 2 teaspoons salt, rosemary, thyme and 18 teaspoon pepper and simmer until celery is tender. Add water chestnuts and flour. Stir until evenly mixed.

Place hens on a tray, skin side down. Brush evenly with 2 tablespoons butter and sprinkle with 3 teaspoons salt and 14 teaspoon pepper. Broil 12-15 minutes. Remove hens from tray and spread dressing over bottom.

Place hens on top and brush top sides with 2 tablespoons melted butter. Return to broiler for another 15 minutes, until golden brown and tender.

Makes: 8 servings

From an old cookbook TURKEY DUCK WILD GAME

7. ROAST PHEASANT WITH CRANBERRIES

ROAST PHEASANT WITH CRANBERRIES

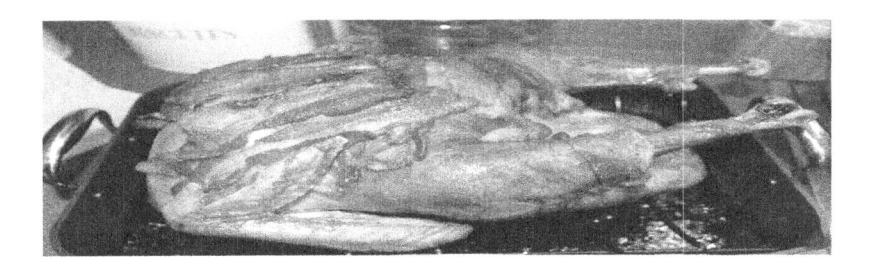

Ingredients:

3 plump hen pheasants
3 teaspoons salt
1/2 teaspoon freshly ground pepper
3 small bay leaves
1 1/2 cloves garlic
3 cloves
3 thick slices onion
3 slices lemon
6 tablespoons chopped celery leaves
3 tablespoons chopped parsley
6 thick slices bacon or larding fat
8 small white onions
2 cups chicken broth
2 tablespoons lemon juice or 1/4 cup Madeira
Flour
1 cup Spiced Cranberries
1/3 cup red currant jelly
2 cups mushrooms

Preparation:

Wash the pheasants and giblets. Set giblets aside. Rub inside and out with 2 teaspoons salt and 1/8: teaspoon pepper. Inside each bird place 1 bay leaf, 1/2 clove garlic, 1 clove, 1 onion slice, 1 lemon slice, 2 tablespoons chopped celery leaves and 1 tablespoon chOpped parsley. Cover the breast of each bird with 2 slices bacon or larding fat. Truss and set in roasting pan. Put the giblets and white onions around the birds. Pour the chicken broth and lemon juice or Madeira over the birds and sprinkle with 1 teaspoon salt and 1/8 teaspoon pepper. Cover and roast in a preheated oven @350° for about 60 minutes. Uncover and remove the fat or bacon and continue roasting until well browned and tender, about 15 minutes longer. Remove birds to a warm platter. Strain broth and remove excess fat. Thicken with a little hour and water paste, add the cranberries and their juice and the currant jelly. Add a little Madeira to the sauce if you wish. Pour over birds and garnish to taste with sautéed mushrooms.

Makes: 6 servings

8. ROAST TURKEY IN FOIL

ROAST TURKEY IN FOIL

Ingredients:

1 turkey
Salt
Monosodium glutamate (optional)
Water
Melted butter
Cranberries
Stuffing

Preparation:
 Rub turkey inside and out with salt and a little monosodium glutamate, if you wish. Fill neck and body cavities with your favorite stuffing. Sew up cavities or fasten with poultry pins or close by sewing with using good cord for cooking, Tie legs

together fasten legs to tail of bird. Wrap the bird in a tight covering of aluminum foil. Put the turkey, breast side down, in a roasting pan for the first hour of roasting and turn it breast side up for the rest of the time, you might tuck in the wings back and under to add support while cooking. Have a small quantity of water in the bottom of the roasting pan at all times. Cooking times may vary but usually allow for 22 minutes per pound in a preheated oven @350°. You can test by inserting a skewer into the fleshy part of the thigh. If the skewer goes in easily and the juice that flows out is clear and not all pink, the bird is cooked. About 30 minutes before cooking time is up, remove foil from the turkey, baste well with melted butter and put in a preheated oven @400° until the skin is a golden brown. It should not be hard or dried out. Serve on a large platter add cranberries. Make gravy from the pan drippings and serve in gravy boat.

9. TURKEY BROILER WITH PECAN STUFF

TURKEY BROILER WITH PECAN STUFF

Ingredients:

1 (6 lb.) turkey broiler
Melted butter
1/2 teaspoon salt
1/8 teaspoon pepper
1/4 teaspoon poultry seasoning

Stuffing:
2 medium onions chopped
1/4 cup butter
1 loaf unsliced day-old white bread
1/2 cup finely chopped pecans
1 tablespoon sage
3/4 cup chopped celery
2 teaspoons salt
1/4 teaspoon pepper
1/4 cup chicken broth

Preparation:

Have the turkey split in half lengthwise. Cut on wing tips. Skewer the legs to the body and brush well with melted butter. Season each half with 1/2 teaspoon salt and pepper. Rub poultry seasoning inside and out.

Stuffing: In a large saucepan over medium heat sauté the onions in butter until they are softened and transparent.

Remove crusts from the bread and pull the crumbs from the center of the loaf. Toast the crumbs lightly and mix with the onions. Add the pecans, sage, celery, salt, pepper and chicken broth. Mix thoroughly. Put the turkey stuffing in the broiler pan and cover with the broiler rack. Place the turkey halves over the stuffing on the rack, skin side down. Place under the broiler 7 inches from the heat. Broil slowly for an hour under medium broiler heat. Turn and brush with melted butter several times. Cook until the thick part of the drumstick is very tender. Make gravy if you wish from the pan drippings.

Makes: 6 servings

10. TURKEY WITH MUSHROOM DRESSING

TURKEY WITH MUSHROOM DRESSING

Ingredients:

1 (8 lb.) turkey cut into portion size pieces
2 tablespoons butter
1/2 teaspoon seasoned salt
1/2 teaspoon meat tenderizer
1/4 teaspoon pepper

Dressing:
4 cups chopped mushrooms
4 cups chopped celery
1/2 cup chicken broth
2 teaspoons salt
1 teaspoon rosemary
1/2 teaspoon thyme
1/8 teaspoon pepper
3/4 cup water chestnuts chopped
1/4 cup flour

Preparation:

Melt the butter in a shallow roasting pan. Add seasoned salt, meat tenderizer and pepper. Rub the turkey pieces with this seasoning. Broil for 20 minutes, until golden and bubbly. Cover with aluminum foil and bake an hour in preheated oven @375°.
Meanwhile, make the dressing. Cook the mushrooms and celery in chicken broth with 2

teaspoons salt, rosemary, thyme and pepper until tender. Remove from heat and stir in the water chestnuts and flour. Put the dressing in a large shallow casserole with the pieces of turkey on top and add any pan juices. Cover the casserole and bake another 60 minutes in a preheated oven @350°. You should remove the cover for the last 10-15 minutes of cooking to brown the top .

Makes: 6 to 8 servings

11. TURKEY HASH

TURKEY HASH

Ingredients:

2 cups leftover turkey chopped medium fine
2 cups chopped boiled potato
1 teaspoon salt
1/8 teaspoon pepper
2 tablespoons butter
1/2 cup cream

Preparation:
Combine the turkey and potato. Mix and season with salt and pepper. In a large saucepan over medium heat brown the mixture in butter. Add the cream, re-season to taste, and cook until cream is well blended and absorbed.

Makes: 4 servings

From an old cookbook TURKEY DUCK WILD GAME

12. BARBECUED TURKEY BROILERS

BARBECUED TURKEY BROILERS

Ingredients:

2 (4 lb.) young turkeys quartered
2 teaspoons salt
1/2 teaspoon pepper
1 teaspoon monosodium glutamate
2 cups butter
6 tablespoons tomato sauce
1 chicken bouillon cube
2 tablespoons grated onion
1 tablespoon Worcestershire sauce
1/2 teaspoon dry mustard
1 teaspoon chili powder
1/4 teaspoon oregano or marjoram

Preparation:

Sprinkle the turkeys with 1 teaspoon salt, 1/4 teaspoon pepper and 1 teaspoon monosodium glutamate and let them stand at room temperature while you make the sauce. Put 1 cup butter, tomato sauce, chicken bouillon cube, grated onion, Worcestershire sauce, mustard, 1 teaspoon salt, M: teaspoon pepper, 1 1/2 teaspoon monosodium glutamate, chili powder and oregano or marjoram into a saucepan. Heat until well blended. Place the turkeys, skin side down, on the pan 5 inches away from the broiling unit. Broil for 10 minutes under medium heat, basting with % cup melted butter. Then move up so that the broilers are only 3 inches away from the unit. Baste again, with pan drippings, and broil for 15 minutes more. Now baste with the barbecue sauce and continue broiling for 5 minutes. Turn the turkeys and baste with another 1A cup melted butter. If the broilers are cooking too fast, move them back to 5 inches away from the heat and broil for 20 minutes more. Baste several times with barbecue sauce. Broil until the turkeys are tender, about another 20 minutes. Serve the remainder of the barbecue sauce on the side.

Makes: 8 servings

13. CURRIED TURKEY AMANDINE

CURRIED TURKEY AMANDINE

Ingredients
:
1 (3 lb.) turkey
5 cups water
4 teaspoons salt
1/2 cup butter
10 tablespoons flour
4 teaspoons curry
Pinch saffron
1 cup white seedless raisins
1/2 cup sherry (optional)
1 clove garlic crushed (optional)
1 cup cooked sliced fresh mushrooms
6 oz. toasted slivered almonds

Preparation:
 Put the turkey in a kettle with water and salt. Cover, bring to a boil, lower heat and poach about 2

hours until tender. Remove turkey, strain the broth and chill. Remove fat from broth. Take the skin, bones and gristle from the turkey and cut into bite-size cubes. You should have 6 cups. Melt the butter and blend in the flour. Add the curry, saffron, 5 cups turkey broth and the raisins. Substitute 1/2 cup sherry for 1/4 cup broth and add the garlic if you wish. Cook 'stirring constantly, until sauce is thick and boiling. Now add the turkey and the drained mushrooms; keep hot until serving time. Put the turkey in a chafing dish or some dish which can be kept hot and served on a buffet. Garnish with toasted almonds.

Makes: 10 to 12 servings

14. SPAGHETTI TURKEY CASSEROLE

SPAGHETTI TURKEY CASSEROLE

Ingredients:

1 1/2 cups diced cooked turkey
1 cup chopped celery
1/4 cup chopped onion
3 tablespoons chopped green pepper
3 tablespoons butter
1 1/2 cups turkey gravy
1 cup chicken broth or any combination of the gravy and broth
1/2 cup cream
1 teaspoon salt
1/8 teaspoon Dash pepper
1 (8 oz.) package spaghetti
1/2 cup bread crumbs seasoned

Preparation:

In a large saucepan over medium heat sauté celery, onion and green pepper in the butter add the 2 1/2 cups gravy and broth, cream, salt, pepper and the turkey.

Cook the spaghetti according to directions on the package. Combine spaghetti and sauce in a casserole. Sprinkle with crumbs, and bake in preheated oven @350° for 30 minutes.

Makes: 6 servings

15. TURKEY GLACE

TURKEY GLACE

Ingredients:

6 cups cooked turkey cut into bite size pieces
6 cups day-old bread cut into cubed (no crusts)
3/4 cup butter
3 teaspoons salt
1 teaspoon thyme
1 teaspoon poultry seasoning
1 cup finely chopped onion
V2 cup flour
2 cups turkey or chicken broth or both
1/4 cup chopped parsley
2 (10 oz.) cans whole cranberry sauce

Preparation:
 In a large saucepan over medium heat sauté the bread cubes in 1/4 cup butter. Season with 1 teaspoon salt, 1/2 teaspoon thyme and 1/2 teaspoon poultry seasoning. Spread on the bottom of a shallow baking dish, 13 1/2 X8 1/2 x 2 inches. Spread the cooked turkey over the bread cubes. Sauté the chopped onion in 1/2 cup butter, add the flour and the turkey or chicken broth or part broth and part gravy, seasoned with 2 teaspoons salt, 1/2 teaspoon thyme, 1/2 teaspoon poultry seasoning and the chopped parsley. Pour this over the turkey and bread cubes. Bake in a preheated oven @350° for 20 minutes. Then take it from the oven and

spread the top with the cranberry sauce. Bake for another 10 minutes.

Makes: 12 servings

16. OYSTER HAM STUFFING

OYSTER HAM STUFFING

Ingredients:

Proceed as for Chestnut Stuffing, substituting a dozen large oysters or 2 dozen small oysters for the chestnuts. Cut the oysters up and add to the bread mixture, together with 1/2 pound of uncooked ham slivered. Reduce the salt to 1 teaspoon to start with and adjust to taste. The amount will depend upon how salty the ham is. Substitute other herbs for the basil and marjoram to taste.

17. CORN-BREAD OYSTER STUFFING

CORN-BREAD OYSTER STUFFING

Ingredients:

1/2 cup coarsely chopped drained oysters
2 cups unsweetened corn-bread crumbs
1/2 cup diced celery
1/4 cup melted butter
2 tablespoons chopped onion
1/4 teaspoon salt
1/2 teaspoon poultry seasoning
1/8 teaspoonDash pepper
1 egg

Preparation:
Mix the com-bread crumbs with the celery, butter, onion, M: teaspoon salt, poultry seasoning and a dash of pepper. Beat the egg slightly and add the crumbs, tossing lightly with a fork. Stir in the oysters. Stuff the bird lightly.

Makes: Enough for a 4-5 pound capon or roasting chicken.

18. POLONAISE BREAD STUFFING

POLONAISE BREAD STUFFING

Ingredients:

1 loaf dry sliced bread
1 cup water
1/2 cup milk
1 large onion chopped
2 tablespoons chopped parsley
1 hard-cooked egg chopped
3 tablespoons shortening
2 eggs
1 teaspoon dill
1 1/2 teaspoons salt
1/4 teaspoon pepper

Preparation:
Crumble the bread and soak the crumbs (2/3 cups) in the water and milk. Beat with a fork. Add the onion, parsley, hard-cooked egg, melted shortening, beaten eggs and dill. Mix very thoroughly and season well with salt and pepper. StuE the chicken and roast as usual.

Makes: Enough for a 31/2-4 pound roasting turkey or chicken

19. CHICKEN-LIVER RICE STUFFING

CHICKEN-LIVER RICE STUFFING

Ingredients:

3-4 chicken livers
6 tablespoons butter
1/3 cup minced onion
1/4 cup minced celery
2 tablespoons minced parsley
1 (5 oz.) package precooked rice
2 teaspoons salt
lls teaspoon pepper
1/2 teaspoon monosodium glutamate
I 1/2 teaspoons poultry seasoning
1 cup boiling water

Preparation:
In a large saucepan over medium heat sauté the chicken livers in 2 tablespoons butter. When cooked through, remove and chop up fine. Mix together the onion, celery and parsley. Add 1/4 cup butter to the pan and, when melted, add the rice, vegetable mixture and chicken livers. Stir over low heat a few minutes and season with salt, pepper, monosodium glutamate and poultry seasoning. Add the boiling water and stir gently over low heat until the liquid is absorbed. Do not completely cook the rice. Stuff the capon and roast as usual.

Makes: Enough for a for a 5-6 pound capon

20. CORN BREAD STUFFING

CORN BREAD STUFFING

Ingredients:

1 pound bulk pork sausage
2 tablespoons water
1 1/4 cups onion diced
1 cup celery diced
1 teaspoon poultry seasoning
1 teaspoon salt
8 cups crumbled unsweetened Corn Bread

Preparation:
Cook the sausage in a frying pan with the water over low heat. When the sausage is cooked, remove meat and sauté the onion and celery in the sausage fat. Add the poultry seasoning and salt. Mix this with the corn bread. Stuff bird lightly.

Makes: Enough for a 12-15 pound turkey

21. WHEAT PILAF STUFFING

WHEAT PILAF STUFFING

Ingredients:

3/4 cup minced scallion or onion
1/2 cup butter
3 cups cracked wheat
6 cups chicken broth
1 1/2 teaspoons salt
1 1/2 teaspoons thyme
1 1/2 teaspoons sage
1/4 teaspoon pepper
3/4 cup plumped white raisins or I 1/2 cups peeled, cored and diced apple
1/2 cup chopped walnuts or toasted blanched almonds (optional)

Preparation:

In a large saucepan over medium heat sauté the scallion or onion in butter until barely tender, about 3 minutes. Add the cracked wheat and cook until golden, 5-10 minutes. Add the broth, salt, thyme, sage and pepper. Cover and simmer 20 minutes. Remove from heat and add raisins or apples and, if you wish, the nuts. If you are going to use this stulfing in a goose or duck, just substitute orange juice for 1/3 of the broth.

Makes: Enough for a 12-14 pound bird:

22. TURKEY DIVAN

TURKEY DIVAN

Ingredients:

Sliced leftover turkey for 6 people
1 bunch broccoli
1 teaspoon salt
1/4 teaspoon pepper
1/4 cup grated Parmesan cheese
3 cups Medium Cream Sauce

Preparation:

Cut the broccoli into slices lengthwise. Cook, drain and arrange in a layer in a shallow casserole. Season with the salt and pepper. Cover broccoli with slices of turkey. Add 1/4 cup Parmesan cheese to the cream sauce, and pour over turkey. Sprinkle the remaining cheese on top and put the casserole under the broiler not too near the heat. When sauce bubbles and is brown it is ready.

Makes: 6 servings

23. SQUABS WITH BLACK OLIVES

SQUABS WITH BLACK OLIVES

Ingredients:

6 squabs
2 teaspoons salt
Stuffing
1 tablespoon butter
} onion chopped fine
1 carrot grated
1 clove garlic crushed
1 bread day-old cut in pieces
Milk
2 eggs
1/3 cup celery leaves chopped
1/4 cup chopped parsley
Grated rind 1/2 orange
1/2 teaspoon salt
1/2 teaspoon poultry seasoning
1/8 teaspoon nutmeg
1/8 teaspoon pepper
12-18 slices bacon
2 (7 1/2 oz.) cans unpitted black olives
Preserved kumquats (garnish)
Parsley (garnish)

Preparation:
 Rub inside cavities of the squabs lightly with salt. Stuffing: In a large saucepan over medium heat sauté the onion the in butter, add carrots and garlic cook until tender. Dip the bread pieces into milk and

squeeze almost dry. Prepare enough to make 2 cups of moistened small pieces. Mix together the bread, onion mixture, eggs, celery leaves, parsley, orange rind, salt, poultry seasoning, nutmeg and pepper. Stuff the birds, fold wings and neck skin under the birds, and then skewer cavities shut. Place birds in large baking pan, top each with 2 or 3 slices of bacon and pour the black olives and juice over all. Bake in a preheated oven @350° basting frequently for until birds are browned and leg joints move easily. If necessary, add more black olive juice (saving olives for garnish). Serve garnished with black olives, kumquats and parsley.

Makes: 6 servings

From an old cookbook TURKEY DUCK WILD GAME

24. Garnishes appropriate to CHICKEN (WHITE-MEAT BIRDS) TURKEY

Herbs, Stuffings, and Garnishes appropriate to CHICKEN (WHITE-MEAT BIRDS) TURKEY

Traditional:
Sage, Cranberry Sauce

Herbs and Spices	Stuffing	Garnishes
Basil Parsley
Bay leaf
Rosemary
Curry
Saffron
Ginger
Savory
Paprika
Tarragon	Celery
Mushrooms
Oregano
Parsley
Sage
Thyme	Chutney
Cranberry sauce
Jelly
Lemon
Oranges
Parsley
Soy sauce

25. ROAST DUCK WITH ORANGE SAUCE

ROAST DUCK WITH ORANGE SAUCE

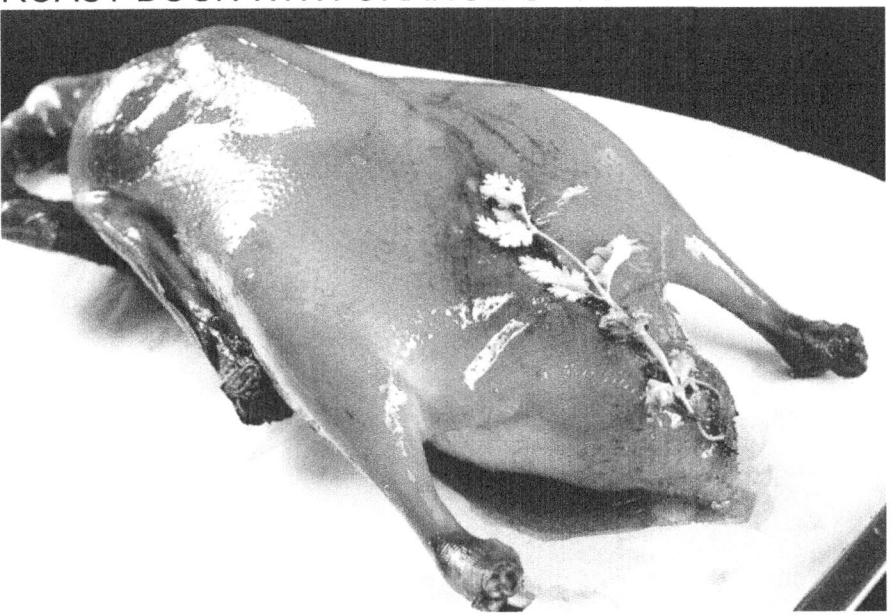

Ingredients:

2 (4-5 lb.) ducks
2 teaspoons salt
1/4 teaspoon pepper
2 onions chopped
2 apples cored and chopped
2 stalks celery chopped
1 1/2 cups orange juice
1/4 cup grape juice (optional)
2 tablespoons flour
2 tablespoons thin slivers orange rind

Preparation:
 Rub the insides of the ducks with 1 teaspoon salt and 1/8 teaspoon pepper. Stulf with mixture of

onions, apples and celery. Skewer and truss the ducks and rub all over with 1 teaspoon salt and 1/8 teaspoon pepper. Place in open roasting pan. Prick the breasts with a fork to release fat in the bird. Roast in preheated oven @400° for 20-25 minutes per pound. You might use a little higher temperature at first to brown the ducks then reduce heat. If you prefer roast in preheated oven @350° about 2 hours baste occasionally. After they are brown, continue baste with a combination of 1/2 cup orange and grape juice to taste. When ducks are tender, drain off the fat and put ducks on platter and keep hot. Make a sauce with 2 tablespoons of the fat, hour, 1 1/2 cups pan juices and 1 cup orange juice. If not enough pan juice, add water or orange juice. Add the orange rind. Cook until slightly thickened. Adjust seasoning. Serve while hot.

Makes: 6 to 8 servings

26. ROAST DUCKLING PIQUANTE

ROAST DUCKLING PIQUANTE

Ingredients:

3 (4 lb.) young ducklings quartered
3 green peppers cut in pieces
3 carrots cut in pieces
3 stalks celery cut in pieces
8 sprigs parsley
3 tablespoons lemon juice
4 1/2 cups consommé
18-20 fillets of anchovy drained
6 tablespoons cornstarch
Brandy (optional)

Preparation:
Arrange the pieces of duckling on a rack in an open roasting pan and roast in a preheated oven @350° until tender about 2 hours, depending on the weight and youth of the birds. Turn frequently, and prick the skin even more frequently to make sure all the fat gets out. While the ducks are roasting, in a large saucepan over medium heat sauté the peppers, carrots and celery for 3 minutes in a little fat poured off the ducklings. Add the parsley, lemon juice, consommé and drained anchovies. Cover and simmer until the vegetables are tender: then strain the broth. Remove ducklings from oven and drain on paper toweling. Dram fat from pan. Skim off any excess fat and thicken the broth with the cornstarch moistened with a little water and, if you wish, add

flavor with a little brandy. Taste for salt the anchovies will probably have supplied more than enough. Put ducklings back in roasting pan. Cover with sauce. Turn off oven. Let duck and sauce stand together in a warm oven for 15-20 minutes before serving.

Makes: 12 servings

27. SWEET AND SOUR ROAST DUCK

SWEET AND SOUR ROAST DUCK

Ingredients:

1 (5-6 lb.) duck
2 teaspoons salt
1 tablespoon monosodium glutamate
I (1 lb. 14 oz.) can pineapple chunks
2 cloves garlic crushed
1 tablespoon soy sauce
4-5 carrots cut in cubed pieces
2-3 green peppers cut in cubed pieces
2 tablespoons cornstarch
1 head celery cabbage shredded
1/2 cup crushed walnuts
Butter

Preparation:
Rub the duck with salt and monosodium glutamate inside and out. Secure the neck opening tightly; sewing is the best way; poultry pins will leave places for the juices to escape. Drain the sirup from the pineapple and pour into the cavity of the duck. Put duck on a rack in a roasting pan and tilt it so that the sirup cannot run out. Add a little water to the roasting pan. Cover and bring to a boil. Lower heat and steam until tender, about 20 minutes to the pound. Add a little water from time to time and keep it steaming. For the last half hour haste frequently. Remove duck, drain pineapple syrup and set duck, breast side down, in an Open pan.

Put it in a preheated oven @500°. When back has browned, turn over and brown the top side. Remove from oven and cool slightly. Take meat from bones in large bite-size pieces. Add bones to broth and pineapple syrup which you have poured from the duck cavity. Add a little more water and cook for 45 minutes. Strain broth into a bowl-there should be 3 1/4 cups. Chill to bring grease to top and skim. All this may be done the day before. Put the pieces of duck into a preheated oven @250° to keep warm. Empty skimmed broth into a saucepan, add garlic and soy sauce and bring to a boil. Add carrots, pineapple and green peppers and cook for 3-4 minutes. Taste for seasoning and add more soy sauce continuously. Stir in cornstarch mixed with a little cold water and continue stirring until sauce is thick and bubbling. Put a layer of shredded cabbage (Chinese cabbage) in the bottom of a casserole or serving dish. Add the hot pieces of duck and pour sauce over all. Top with walnuts, sautéed in a little butter until crisp.

Makes: 6 servings

28. PINEAPPLE DUCK (Chinese Duck)

PINEAPPLE DUCK (Chinese Duck)

Ingredients:

1 (4 lb.) duckling cut up
1 teaspoon salt
1/4 teaspoon pepper
4 slices pineapple cut into 1-inch pieces
1 green pepper cut into 8 pieces
2 tablespoons cornstarch
1/4 cup cold water
2 teaspoons soy sauce
Rice

Preparation:

Put the duckling into a kettle with boiling water to cover and simmer for an hour. Remove duck from broth, skim and set aside. In a large heavy skillet warm a tablespoon of fat skimmed from the broth. Brown the pieces of duck on all sides. Season with salt and pepper. Add 1% cups of duck broth and the pineapple and green pepper. Cover and cook over moderate heat for 10 minutes. Blend the cornstarch with water and soy sauce. Stir into the mixture in the skillet and cook until thickened, stirring constantly. Serve with rice.

Makes: 4 servings

29. PLANKED DUCKLING

PLANKED DUCKLING

Ingredients:

2 (2 1/2 lb.) young ducklings split and quartered
2 1/2 teaspoons salt
1/4 teaspoon pepper
6-8 sweet potatoes peeled
7 tablespoons butter
1 pound white onions
8 large pitted cooked prunes (garnish)
1 (3 oz.) package cream cheese (garnish)
1/2 teaspoon grated orange rind (garnish)
Few drops hot pepper sauce (garnish)

Preparation:

Sprinkle ducklings with 3/4 teaspoon salt and 1/8 teaspoon pepper and place, skin side down, on broiler rack. Broil under moderate heat. While the duck is cooking, boil the sweet potatoes I per person-and mash them. Season with 1 teaspoon salt, 1/8 teaspoon pepper and 1/4: cup butter. Cook the white onions until just tender. Season with 1/2 teaspoon salt and dash pepper, and toss them in 3 tablespoons melted butter. For garnish, stuff the prunes with a little seasoned cream cheese. Mix the softened cream cheese with 1/4 teaspoon salt, the orange rind, dash pepper and 2 drops hot pepper sauce. When duck is tender, arrange in the center of a large plank. Surround with an edge of the mashed sweet potatoes, and garnish with the onions and stuffed prunes. Put in a preheated oven @450° for 15 minutes, to brown the onions.

Makes: 6 to 8 servings

30. DUCK IN CASSEROLE

DUCK IN CASSEROLE

Ingredients:

2 (5 lb.) ducks or 3 smaller ducklings
2 teaspoons salt
1/4 teaspoon pepper
1 teaspoon monosodium glutamate
3 cups water

Sauce:
Rind I seedless orange cut into strips
1 cup orange juice
2 tablespoons lemon juice
1 tablespoon grated orange rind
1/2 cup currant jelly
1 clove garlic crushed (optional)
3 tablespoons cornstarch
3 tablespoons water
Preserved kumquats (garnish)
Parsley (garnish)

Preparation:

Rub the ducks inside and out with salt, pepper and monosodium glutamate, and roast in a preheated oven @325° until tender, takes about 30 minutes per pound. When skin becomes dry, prick with fork to let fat run out. Cook giblets and necks in salted water. When ducks are done, remove from pan to cool. Remove as much fat from pan as possible, leaving the drippings. Add a little water to pan and boil on top of range, scraping bottom of pan. Add 2 cups strained broth from giblets and refrigerate. Cut duck from bones into bite-size pieces. Put ducks in a lO-cup casserole. Heat in a preheated oven @350° until sauce is ready. Sauce:

Cover the julienne orange strips with water, bring to boil and drain. Repeat twice to eliminate bitter taste. The duck and blanched orange rind may be prepared in advance. Add the orange juice, lemon juice, grated orange rind and julienne strips of orange rind. Next put in the currant jelly, garlic if you like, and thicken with cornstarch blended with water. Cook, stirring until sauce thickens. Pour sauce over the ducks and garnish with kumquats and parsley.

Makes: 8 to 10 servings

31. DUCK WITH APPLE SAUERKRAUT STUFFING

DUCK WITH APPLE SAUERKRAUT STUFFING

Ingredients:

2 (4-5 lb.) ducks
1 teaspoon salt
1/4 teaspoon pepper

Stuffing:
3/4 cup salt pork diced
2 onions chopped
4 large tart apples peeled, cored and diced
2 1/2 teaspoons salt
1/8 teaspoons pepper
1/2 teaspoon thyme
I 1/2 teaspoons caraway seed
30 oz. sauerkraut in jars or cans

Preparation:
Rub the cavities of both of the ducks with salt and pepper. To make the striding, heat the salt pork until transparent. Add the onions and apples and cook until tender. Season with salt, pepper, thyme and caraway seed. Remove from heat. Toss in the drained sauerkraut and mix. Pack the stuffing into the birds and truss. Prick the birds well with a sharp fork, and prick several times while roasting. Place ducks on a trivet in roasting pan and roast for 2 1/2 hours in a preheated oven @350° about 22 minutes

per pound. Cooking time depends upon the size and age of the ducks.

Makes: 8 servings

32. BROILED DUCKLING

BROILED DUCKLING

Ingredients:

2 (2-31/2 lb.) young ducklings
2 teaspoons salt
1/4 teaspoon pepper

Preparation:
Select young tender birds, which are the easiest to broil most of the time. Split and quarter the birds. Sprinkle with salt and pepper, and place, skin side down, on broiler rack. Broil under moderate heat until brown and tender. During the broiling time, turn the pieces several times, pricking occasionally to let fat out. Basting is not usually necessary as duckling is more fatty than chicken.

Makes: 6 servings

33. ROAST DUCK WITH ORANGE STUFFING

ROAST DUCK WITH ORANGE STUFFING

Ingredients:

2 (4 lb.) ducks
1 teaspoon salt
5 orange halves Stuffing
10 slices raisin bread
1 1/2 cups diced celery
2 oranges or 3 tangerines
2 teaspoons grated orange or tangerine rind
1 teaspoon salt
1/4 teaspoon thyme

Gravy:
1 cup water
1 cup orange iuice
2 tablespoons cornstarch
1 teaspoon molasses
2 teaspoons soy sauce
1/2 teaspoon salt
1/8 teaspoon pepper
1/2 cup slivered blanched almonds
2 tablespoons butter
Preserved kumquats (garnish)
Tangerine sections (garnish)

Rub the ducks with salt inside and out.

Stuffing: Cut the crusts from the raisin bread, toast and break into small pieces. Add the celery. Section and seed the oranges or tangerines. Mix with the bread and celery and add the grated orange or tangerine rind. Season with salt and thyme.

Stuff the ducks and skewer and truss them. Arrange the ducks on a rack in an open roasting pan. Prick ducks well with a fork. Roast in preheated oven @325° for 2 1/2 hours or 22 minutes per pound, draining off the fat every half hour and basting each time by squeezing half an orange over the birds. Rub the skin with the squeezed orange half and leave the orange skins in the pan near the ducks during the roasting to add flavor to the gravy.

Gravy: Drain off all but 1 tablespoon fat. Add the water and any juice to the drippings and scrape loose all brown pieces stuck to the pan. Mix the orange juice and cornstarch until smooth. Add to gravy. Cook, stirring constantly, until as thick as heavy cream. Add molasses and soy sauce and season to taste with salt and pepper. Brown the almonds in the butter. Drain on paper toweling. Add to gravy just before serving with the duck. Garnish the duck with kumquats and tangerine sections if you wish.

Makes: 8 servings

These ducks may be stuffed with Wild Rice, Wheat Pilaf or your favorite stuffing.

34. DUCKUNG BIGARADE

DUCKUNG BIGARADE

3 (4 lb.) ducklings dressed and quartered
6 oranges
3 tablespoons sugar
3 tablespoons vinegar
3 cups chicken broth
3 cups orange juice
2 tablespoons lemon juice
1 tablespoon grated orange rind
1 1/2 teaspoons salt
1/4 teaspoon pepper
1/4 cup cornstarch
1/2 cup cold water
Orange wedges (garnish)

Preparation:
In a roast pan put ducklings in a preheated oven @350° for 2 hours or 22 minutes per pound, depending on weight and youth of birds. Turn and prick skin very frequently to make sure all fat gets out. After first half hour of roasting, place partly squeezed orange halves on each piece of duckling. Save the juice. Remove orange halves half an hour before the end of roasting. About the same time start to make the sauce. Put the sugar and vinegar into a saucepan and cook until the mixture caramelizes. Do not allow to burn. Add chicken broth, orange juice, lemon juice, orange rind, salt and pepper. Mix well and keep warm over low heat.

When duckling is tender to the fork, remove from oven and drain on paper toweling. Place skin side down in a baking pan and pour hot sauce over duckling. Return pan to the oven @350° for another 5 minutes and keep basting. Drain sauce back into saucepan. Keep duckling warm.

Sauce: Mix cornstarch with cold water and add to the sauce. Cook and stir until smooth and thickened. Arrange duckling on a large platter and spoon some of the sauce over each piece. Garnish with orange sections. Serve the remaining sauce in a gravy boat.

Makes: 12 servings

35. ROAST GOOSE WITH PRUNE STUFFING

ROAST GOOSE WITH PRUNE STUFFING

Ingredients:

1 (12-14 lb.) goose

Stuffing:
9 cups the bread crumbs
3/4 cup chopped onion
2 1/2 cups tart apple peeled, cored and diced
2 1/4 teaspoons salt
2 teaspoons poultry seasoning
3/4 pound tenderized prunes pitted and cut into small pieces
6 tablespoons butter melted
Flour

Preparation:

Goose contains a great deal more fat than chicken and turkey, so allow 1 1/2 pounds per person. To make the stuffing, mix the bread crumbs with chopped onion, apple, salt, poultry seasoning and prunes. Moisten with the butter and mix well. Stuff the goose very loosely with the prune stuffing. Pull back the ,skin over the neck and fasten with a poultry pin or sew with cord after you have stuffed the cavity. Truss and place the goose on a rack tuck the wing back and down to help keep bird from moving while cooking. Roast in preheated oven @325° for 20-25 minutes per pound, give about 4 hours. Remember to prick skin to allow fat to escape and skim off the fat as it accumulates in the pan. To be sure the goose is done, test by moving the drumsticks, which should be loose and move easily. Place on heated platter.

Make gravy from the drippings in the pan with flour and stock made by cooking the neck and giblets in a cup of salted water.

Makes: 8 to 10 servings

36. ROAST GOOSE

ROAST GOOSE

Ingredients:

1 (15-20 lb.) goose
2 teaspoons salt
1/4 teaspoon pepper
1 1/2 cups orange juice
4 tablespoons flour
Wild Rice or Chestnut Stuffing
or Wheat Pilaf
2 cups water or chicken broth (optional)

Preparation:
A goose is an extremely fat bird and pounds will melt away in roasting, in addition to the fat you pull out of the bird interior. A 20 pound goose will serve 12 people. Allow at least 1 1/2 pounds per person. Remove as much loose fat from the insides of the goose as you can. Rub inside and out with salt and pepper. Fill with wild rice or other stuffing such as Wheat Pilaf or chestnut stuffing. The goose's liver should be prepared separately and served as the delicious foie gras, as its name sake. Truss the goose and place on a rack in an open roasting pan. Roast in preheated oven @325° for 20 to 25 minutes per pound 4-5 hours. Prick the skin every half hour to let the fat run out. Ladle off excess fat as it accumulates. For the last two hours baste with a little orange juice each time you prick the skin. To make gravy, place goose on a warm platter. Quick

sauce remove most of the fat from the pan. Blend in some flour, add 2 cups water or chicken broth. Adjust seasoning to taste.

Makes: 10 to 12 servings

37. POACHED GOOSE

POACHED GOOSE

Ingredients:

1 (14 lb.) fat young goose
2 carrots
1 onion
Sprig parsley
Few peppercorns
2 teaspoons salt

Stuffing:
2 cloves garlic crushed
4 onions chopped
1 cup finely chopped celery
3 tablespoons butter
3 (7 1/2 oz.) cans minced clams .
3 cups cooked wild rice
1/2 cup milk or clam iuice
5 tablespoons chopped parsley
1 teaspoon rosemary
1 teaspoon freshly ground pepper
2 teaspoons salt

Preparation:

In a large saucepan make the stuffing, over medium heat sauté the garlic, onions and celery in butter until golden brown. Drain the juice from the clams and set aside. Add clams to the saucepan and cook 1 minute, stirring constantly. Mix the contents of the saucepan with the wild rice and add

1/2 cup milk or clam juice or a combination or both. season with parsley, rosemary, pepper and 2 teaspoons salt.

Fill both the neck and body of the goose with stuffing and secure the cavities closed . Enclose the bird in a piece of muslin and sew it or pin with safety pins. Place it, breast down, in a kettle with a tight-fitting lid. Cover with cold water. Add the carrots, onion, parsley, peppercorns and 2 teaspoons salt. Bring to a boil, lower heat and skim. Cover and cook for about 3 hours, until the goose is tender. Add a little water from time to time to keep the same water level. Remove goose from pot and put it, breast side up, in a roasting pan. Strain the broth and cool it quickly and skim off any excess fat. Pour a little broth over the goose to keep it moist. Boil the rest, uncovered, until it is reduced to 3-4 cups. All this may be done the day before if you wish. Before serving, put the goose in a preheated oven @300° for about 90 minutes, until hot. Let skin brown to a golden color under the broiler. Thicken the sauce with flour or serve with Caper Sauce made with the broth instead of oil.

Makes: 8 servings

38. Herbs and Garnishes appropriate to DUCK- GOOSE- SOUAB

Herbs and Garnishes appropriate to DUCK GOOSE SOUAB

Traditional: Sage Tart Jelly

Herbs and Spices	Garnishes
Rosemary Sage Savory Tarragon Thyme Basil Bay leaf Juniper Marjoram Oregano	Celery Kumquats Lemon Orange Pickled peaches Pureed apricots Spiced apples Tart jellv

39. WILD GAME

WILD GAME

You need not be intimidated by wild game in your kitchen, venison is as domesticated as beef, pheasant as easy as chicken. The notable difference is that wild animals are leaner than contented cows and barnyard fowl. They therefore need a blanket of fat before they are cooked such as lard or salt pork. Then, too, they are likely to have developed strong muscles from the exercising they have done, and may require marinating or other tenderizing.

We consume a lot of venison in north america. The name venison comes from the Latin venatio, meaning game or hunting We now use it to mean the flesh of any antlered animal.

Buffalo (bison) is popular: the herds are being raised in the west like cattle. The meat of buffalo "really wild" is stronger and richer than beef, but the tender cuts are cooked in a similar fashion.

Bear meat is rich, sweet, and delicious. It looks like beef, but has the consistency and texture of pork. Bear meat should be cooked throughly, unless it has been frozen for a minimum of two weeks, because of trichinosis. Older animals need tenderizing. Rabbit, even though domesticated, is considered to be game.

40. GAME BIRDS

GAME BIRDS

The most popular game bird is the wild duck, and there is a large variety of species to choose from. Mallards predominate, but there are many others: canvasback, redheads, teal, black, wood, broadbill, pintail, and widgeon.

Wild turkeys are a hunters delight but scarce and therefore hard to find. Wild geese are not easily available either. Young geese are delicious but the old birds tend be tough, a goose can frequently live to a ripe old age of some fifty years. Grouse, quail, partridge,

pheasant, woodcock, snipe, and doves are much more readily available. They all have that rich aromatic smell and unique flavor and need to be well lubricated while cooking to keep its tenderness and flavor and be an exotic meal.

Preparation:
Game birds should be eviscerated as soon as possible. They are easier to pluck while still warm, after they are shot. They should be kept cool until refrigerated. Birds should not be washed, they may be wiped with a damp cloth. Refrigerate for two days before cooking or freezing. Wild fowl gets a lot of exercise and is therefore the meat is much drier than domestic fowl. A little fat maybe required when

cooking these young birds, they can be broiled, fried, or roasted; older ones are better cooked with moisture-braised or stewed. In any case, they should be rubbed with butter or other shortening, or covered with bacon or fat.

41. ROAST WILD DUCK

ROAST WILD DUCK

Ingredients:
1 wild duck
1 onion cut into pieces
2 stalks celery cut into pieces
1 teaspoon salt
1/4 cup butter

Preparation:
  Wipe the birds with a damp cloth and clean very well-do not wash. Singe. Put the pieces of onion and celery into the cavity. Sprinkle the duck with salt and lay it in a shallow pan. Rub soft butter over legs and breast. Roast in a preheated oven @450° for 20 minutes per pound or for well done duck 30 minutes per pound. If you are using a frozen bird, thaw, leave at room temperature before cooking. One duck usually is enough for two people unless it is very small.

Makes: 2 servings

42. ROAST WILD DUCK DELUXE

ROAST WILD DUCK DELUXE

Ingredients:

3. large or 6 small ducks
2 tablespoons bacon drippings
I 1/2 teaspoons salt
1/4 teaspoon pepper
2 apples peeled, cored and coarsely chopped
6-8 slices bacon

Preparation:
Wipe the birds with a damp cloth and clean very well-do not wash. Singe. Rub with bacon drippings and sprinkle, inside and out, with salt and pepper. Fill cavities with the apples. Put 2 slices of bacon over each breast. Roast in preheated oven @450° for 20-25 minutes and haste 2 or 3 times with bacon drippings. If you want the ducks really rare pink meat, serve at once, otherwise, roast another 15-20 minutes with oven at @350° and the birds will still be moist and tinged with pink. For large ducks such as mallards, weighing over 3 pounds, roast 15-18 minutes per pound. Most ducks will serve two even though the breast is usually the only part eaten. Small ducks such as teal, weighing less than a pound, make individual servings.

Makes : 6 servings

43. ROAST MALLARD DUCK

ROAST MALLARD DUCK

Ingredients:
3 large ducks
2 teaspoons salt
1/4 teaspoon pepper
1 cup coarsely chopped celery
1 cup coarsely chopped onion
Bacon fat
1/4 cup butter
1/4 cup hot water
1/2 cup chopped parsley
1/4 cup minced onion
1 clove garlic crushed
1/4 cup orange juice
1 orange rind grated
1/4 cup Madeira, sherry or mixed orange and lemon iuice

Preparation:
  Wipe the ducks with a damp cloth, singe and clean very well. Sprinkle, inside and out, with salt and pepper. Fill cavities with chopped celery and onion. Rub outside with bacon fat. Roast, uncovered, in preheated oven @450° for 15-20 minutes. Baste several times with juices. Reduce heat to 350° and baste with a mixture of melted butter and hot water. Cover and bake for another 20-30 minutes, depending on the size of the ducks. Mix and in a large saucepan over medium heat simmer the parsley, minced onion, garlic, and juice and rind of

orange. Add wine or orange-lemon juice to taste. Pour mixture over the ducks and serve at once if the ducks are tender to the fork. If they are older birds they will need to cook a little longer, in this case, continue roasting for another 30 minutes or until they are tender. Baste regularly. Skim off extra fat from sauce and serve with the sliced breast or serve separately, in heated bowl. It's customary to carve birds at the table.

Makes: 6 servings

44. BREAST OF WILD DUCK-SAUCE BIGARADE

BREAST OF WILD DUCK-SAUCE BIGARADE

Ingredients:

2 wild ducks dressed Bacon slices or salt pork
2 onions chopped coarse
1/2 cup water

Sauce:
1 1/2 cups chicken broth
1/2 teaspoon salt
1/2 teaspoon grated onion
Small piece bay leaf
2-3 peppercorns
1-2 small pieces celery
1 leek or scallion diced
2 sprigs parsley
Pinch thyme
Rind 1 orange slivered
1 tablespoon flour
1/2 teaspoon paprika
Dash cayenne pepper or hot pepper sauce
1/4 cup strained orange juice
Wild Rice or Rice Pilaf

Preparation:
 Lay slices of bacon or salt pork over the breasts of the ducks. Place onions inside the birds. Put in shallow roasting pan with the water to prevent sticking. Roast in preheated oven @500° for 18

minutes. Carefully remove the breasts and set aside.

Sauce: Pour the chicken broth over duck carcasses and legs. Add salt and grated onion. Tie the bay leaf, peppercorns, celery, leek or scallion, parsley and thyme in a square of cheesecloth with a string. This is a bouquet garnie. Add to the broth and simmer an hour. Strain broth, add orange rind and boil 3 minutes in a little water and drain. Smooth the flour into the drippings in the roasting pan for 1 minute over low heat. Add the duck broth, paprika and cayenne or hot pepper sauce. Stir until sauce is smooth and slightly thickened. Strain, add the orange juice and slivered orange rind. Put in the duck breasts and cook 2-3 minutes to heat up the duck. Serve the breasts in the sauce accompanied by wild rice or pilaf.

Makes: 4 servings

45. QUAIL

QUAIL

Ingredients:

l2 quail (2 per person)
6 tablespoons butter
1 teaspoon salt
1/4 teaspoon pepper

Preparation:
Wipe the quail with a damp cloth; do not wash. These are delicate small dry birds. If to be broiled, split, sprinkle with salt and pepper and rub thoroughly with butter. Place skin side down on broiler. Broil for 5 minutes; baste with butter. After 5 more minutes turn, brush with melted butter, and broil another 10 minutes. Total time, 20 minutes.

Makes: 6 servings

46. ROAST QUAIL

ROAST QUAIL

Preparation:
Wipe with damp cloth. Salt and pepper inside and out. Rub generously with butter. In a large casserole dish brown the birds in a preheated oven, 450°- 500° for 15 minutes; reduce to 350°, add a little chicken broth, cover and steam 20 minutes. Quail is a dry bird so baste often with butter and broth. The steaming process keeps them moist and helps retain the distinctive flavor. Try placing a half slice of bacon over the breast and putting a few raisins which have been plumped in hot water inside each bird. Quail is a great delicacy and nothing should be done to destroy the flavor. Two quail per person unless the quail are very large.

47. BREASTS OF PARTRIDGE OR PHEASANT

BREASTS OF PARTRIDGE OR PHEASANT

Ingredients:

Breasts of 2 partridges or pheasants dressed
4 slices ham
1 teaspoon salt
1/4 teaspoon cayenne pepper
1/2 cup butter
1 teaspoon grated onion
1/2 teaspoon rosemary
1/2 lbs. mushrooms sliced thin
2 tablespoons flour
1 cup chicken broth
1/4 cup brandy (optional)

Preparation:
 Cut breasts from bone, leaving skin on. Dust with salt and cayenne. Brown well on both sides in deep butter with onion and rosemary for 8 to 10 minutes. Keep warm in a covered pan in a preheated oven @250° while you sauté bird in same butter. Put 1 breast on each slice of ham. Sauté mushrooms in the same skillet for 3 minutes. Push mushrooms to one side of the pan, pour off all but about 2 tablespoons butter, add flour, blend, and add chicken broth. When sauce is velvety smooth and thick, pour over birds. Adjust seasoning, pour over

the heated brandy and serve flaming. Serve with Currant Jelly or Apricot Puree or any tart jelly.

Makes: 4 servings

48. FRIED PHEASANT

FRIED PHEASANT

Ingredients:

1 young pheasant dressed and cut up
Flour
1 teaspoon salt
1/3 teaspoon pepper
6 tablespoons butter or bacon dripping:

Preparation:
You can tell a young pheasant by the gray color of the feet and the flexibility of the tip of the breastbone. Treat the pheasant as you do fried chicken. Roll the pieces in tlour seasoned with salt and pepper. Fry them in butter or bacon drippings until golden brown and tender, about half an hour.

Makes: 2 to 3 servings

49. GROUSE

GROUSE

About

The North American cousins of the Scotch and British grouse are highly favored at the table except the prairie chicken, which is likely to be tough. Grouse are available to the hunter all over the North America, except in the South and Southeast. Grouse usually weighs from 1 to 1 1/2 pounds and one serves 1 and sometimes 2 people. A young bird has a flexible breastbone tip and very tender meat in the wings. The feet of young birds lighter and not as dark as the older birds.

50. GROUSE BAKED

GROUSE

Ingredients:

4 grouse dressed
Milk
1 teaspoon salt
1/4 teaspoon pepper
8 pieces lemon rind
8 slices bacon

Preparation:
Wash the birds in milk. Drain and pat dry. Season with salt and pepper. Put a strip of lemon rind and a slice of bacon in each cavity. Put one or two birds on a large strip of heavy aluminum foil. Cover the breasts with slices of bacon. Fold over foil and roll edges to make a tight package. Bake in a preheated oven @400° for 20-40 minutes, depending upon the age and size of the birds. Open the foil and brown the grouse for about 10 minutes. Serve with juices.

Makes: 4 to 6 servings

51. BROILED PARTRIDGE

BROILED PARTRIDGE

Ingredients:

2 partridges dressed
1 teaspoon salt
1/3 teaspoon pepper
1/2 cup butter

Preparation:
Split the birds and sprinkle with salt and pepper. Rub thoroughly with 1/4 cup butter. Broil the partridge, breast down, for 15 minutes, basting every few minutes. Then turn over the bird, brush with 1/2 cup melted butter and broil until brown about another 15 minutes. Baste regularly with pan drippings. This bird is a dry one and basting with the butter (or olive oil) is essential.

Makes: 4 servings

52. GROUSE IN CASSEROLE

GROUSE IN CASSEROLE

Ingredients:

4 grouse dressed
Milk
1/2 cup melted butter
1 teaspoon salt
1/4 teaspoon pepper
1 cup cream
1 lemon use the Grated rind
1/4 cup brandy (optional)

Preparation:
Soak the birds in milk for at least an hour. Drain and truss. Place in a casserole with the butter poured over them, brown in preheated oven @450° for 15-20 minutes, basting often. Sprinkle with salt and pepper and pour the cream over the birds. Add lemon rind, and brandy if you wish. Cover and continue baking until done, 20 to 35 minutes. The time will depend entirely upon the age of the birds. Baste several times.

Makes: 4 to 6 servings

53. WILD GOOSE

WILD GOOSE

Preparation:
Goose, unlike other wild birds, is likely to be fat, not dry. You cook it much as you would tame goose, which has even more fat. Sear in a preheated oven @450° to 500° for 15 minutes, reduce heat to 325° and roast, preferably covered, until done, usually about 20 minutes per pound. Baste frequently adding a little water and 1/3 cup orange juice to the juices in the pan. Be sure to skim off excess fat from the roasting pan regularly.

54. VENISON

VENISON

Preparation:
Before eating or freezing venison, hang young deer for a week and older deer for two to three weeks at a temperature of about 38°. The meat may be cooked like beef-steaks and chops broiled or sautéed, legs roasted, and the tougher cuts pot-roasted. Unless you have a very young animal, the meat should be tenderized. The best tenderizer for game is a tasty marinade which draws any unpleasant gamy flavor. Try treating your young deer meat to soak in buttermilk. Any fat should be cut off and replaced with other fat such as salt pork or beef fat. Salt pork is excellent for larding large pieces of meat; smaller pieces may be wrapped in fat. Venison, like beef, may be served rare, medium, or well done.

55. VENISON ROAST

VENISON ROAST

Ingredients:

1 1 (5 lb.) piece venison boned and tied with cord
Salt pork or bacon Marinade
1/2 cup red wine vinegar and 1 cup of water or 1 cup red wine 1/2 cup salad oil
1 bay leaf
1 large clove garlic cut in half
Few juniper berries (optional)
1 teaspoon rosemary or 1/2 teaspoon thyme
1/8 teaspoon freshly ground pepper
1 teaspoon salt

Preparation:

Have the butcher lard the venison with strips of salt pork, or stud with small pieces of pork fat or bacon. Put the venison in a pan or bowl with the marinade. The juniper berries add to the flavor so use them if they are available. Let stand 1-3 days in the refrigerator, turning several times. Put the meat in a roasting pan and cover it with thin slices of salt pork or bacon. Cover and roast in preheated oven @350° for 45 minutes, basting frequently with a little of the marinade. Remove cover and roast for half an hour. This roast should be medium; if you want it rare, cook it a few minutes less. Remove meat to warm platter. Pour off excess fat keep 2 tablespoons for sauce. Add a little flour to the pan and scrape the pan well mix until smooth. Add any of the marinade that is left. Strain the gravy, which should be a rich brown mahogany color.

Makes: 6 to 8 servings

56. VENISON ROAST DELUXE

VENISON ROAST DELUXE (Rehbraten Gretta)

Ingredients:

1 (5 lb.) piece boneless leg of venison
1 quart buttermilk
1/2 pound Bacon sliced
1 teaspoon salt
1/4 teaspoon pepper
4 tablespoons sour cream (optional)
1/4 teaspoon sugar
1/4 cup red wine or 2 tablespoons red wine vinegar

Preparation:
 Soak the venison in buttermilk to cover for 2-3 days, turning once or twice. Remove meat and place in roasting pan, reserving the buttermilk. Cover the meat with bacon and roast, covered, in a moderate oven, 350° for about 20 minutes to the pound. Add a little water and baste frequently. Add more bacon after about 40 minutes, putting it over the top of the roast when you turn it.

If you are using an oven thermometer, the roast will be rare @135° medium @140, and well done @150°. Unless the venison is old and therefore tough, it should be pink if not rare. For the last 15 minutes of cooking, add salt and pepper, remove cover and let the meat brown. To make gravy, remove meat from roaster, scrape all the brown bits from the bottom of the pan into the gravy. Thicken with a little flour and water paste. Add 1/2 cup buttermilk, sour cream, season to taste, sugar and vinegar or wine. If not using sour cream, use 1 cup buttermilk. Strain the gravy.

Makes: 6 to 8 servings

From an old cookbook TURKEY DUCK WILD GAME

57. ROAST SADDLE OF VENISON

ROAST SADDLE OF VENISON

Ingredients:

1 (5-6 lb.) saddle and/or rack of venison
1 large carrot diced
1 large onion diced
1 bunch scallions chopped
1/4 cup olive or salad oil
1 tablespoon tarragon or 1 teaspoon rosemary and pinch cloves
1 tablespoon salt
1/2 teaspoon freshly ground pepper
1/2 cup dry red or white wine or 2 tablespoons red or white wine vinegar
1 clove garlic crushed
1/2 lb salt pork sliced 1/4 inch thick

Preparation:

First make the marinade. In a large skillet over medium heat sauté the carrots, onions and scallions in oil until slightly brown and tender, about 5 minutes. Remove the skillet from heat and add tarragon or rosemary, cloves, salt, pepper and wine or wine vinegar. Red wine or vinegar gives the meat a richer taste, while the white is more likely to preserve the venison flavor. Wipe the meat with a damp cloth to moisten and rub all sides with the garlic. Make a few small slits with a sharp knife and rub the roast thoroughly with the marinade. If the roast has been larded (which is wise to have the butcher do this for you), you do not need to make slits, since the marinade will penetrate through the holes made by larding. Let it stand at least all day

24 to 48 hours is normally the time it takes to marinate venison. Place in a shallow open roasting pan and cover the meat with slices of salt pork. Add a little of the marinade. Roast in a preheated oven @400° for 15 minutes. Add a little more marinade and baste regularly. Reduce heat to 350° and continue to haste every 15 minutes. The roast may be coated in a flour and water dough or aluminum foil. A venison roast does not need to be browned. Roast 10-15 minutes to the pound. If you like it rare, 10 minutes is usually enough time, 15 minutes per pound for well done. To make the gravy, remove roast place in a warm platter, and remove the pieces of fat. Pour off excess fat from pan juices but leave 2 tablespoon to make the sauce, and strain. Thicken with a little flour and water paste, and add the strained marinade and broth or water. Season to taste. Venison should be served with a tart jelly, tart fruit sauce or Chestnut purée.

Makes: 8 to 10 servings

58. VENISON STEW

Ingredients:

3 pounds boneless venison
Flour
1 teaspoon salt
1/2 teaspoon pepper
1/4 cup shortening or bacon dripping:
2 onions chopped
1 clove garlic crushed
6 carrots sliced
1/2 teaspoon basil or 1/2 teaspoon thyme
I cup water
1 cup consommé
1/2 pound mushrooms cut up (optional)

Preparation:
Cut the meat into bite size cubes. Trim off all fat. Roll in the flour seasoned with 1/2 teaspoon salt and 1/4 teaspoon pepper. Sauté in hot shortening or bacon drippings until brown. Add onions, garlic, carrots and basil or thyme. Add a mixture of the water and consommé. Cover and simmer for about an hour. Add the mushrooms, if you wish. Season with 1/2 teaspoon salt and 1/4 teaspoon pepper. Cover and simmer 20-30 minutes, until the meat is very tender. If juice is not thick enough, thicken it with a little flour and water paste.

Makes: 6 servings

59. RABBIT

RABBIT

Notes:
Domestic rabbits, and some imported ones, are available in supermarkets everywhere. These rabbits have a great deal of fine-grained white meat and you may fry or bake them as you would chicken. Semi-domesticated rabbits will vary in age and toughness; treat them accordingly. As with other wild game, older Wild rabbits the meat is likely to be very tough and rubbery.

60. HASENPFEFFER

HASENPFEFFER

Ingredients:

1 (5-6 lb.) rabbit cut into serving portions

Marinade:
2 cups vinegar
2 cups water
1 tablespoon salt
1 teaspoon peppercorns
1 large onion sliced
6 cloves
1 bay leaf
1/2 teaspoon tarragon
1/2 teaspoon basil
1 carrot shredded
1 quart water
1/2 cup finely chopped onion
2 tablespoons butter
2 tablespoons flour
1 tablespoon brown sugar
1/2 cup sour cream
1/2 cup parsley chopped

Preparation:

Place pieces of rabbit in a large bowl and add vinegar, water, salt, peppercorns, onion, cloves, bay leaf, tarragon, basil and carrot. Cover and marinate-for 24 hours in a cool place, turning pieces of rabbit occasionally. Remove meat and shake off excess marinade. If using a frozen rabbit, thaw and marinate for several hours. Place in a large casserole or Dutch oven and add 1 quart water. Cover and simmer until meat is tender, about 2 hours. Remove rabbit and keep warm. Reserve 2 cups broth.

In a large saucepan over medium heat sauté the onion in the butter until tender. Add the flour and brown sugar. Blend in the 2 cups broth and cook until thickened. Adjust seasonings, lower heat and blend in sour cream. Pour over rabbit, sprinkle top with chopped parsley.

Makes: 6 servings

61. BRAISED RABBIT

Ingredients:

1 (3 lb.) young rabbit cut up
1 cup flour
2 teaspoons salt
1/4 teaspoon pepper
6 tablespoons shortening
1 cup chicken broth
3 tablespoons lemon juice
6 tablespoons orange juice
1/4 cup chopped parsley
1 small onion chopped
2 tablespoons minced green pepper
1/8 teaspoon ginger
1 cup sliced mushrooms

Preparation:

Dredge the rabbit pieces with flour, seasoned with 1 teaspoon salt and 1/4 teaspoon pepper. In a large saucepan over medium heat sauté until well browned in the shortening. Drain off excess fat. Add chicken broth, lemon and orange juices, parsley, onion and green pepper. Season with 1 teaspoon salt, 1/8 teaspoon pepper and the ginger. Cover and simmer over low heat until tender, about 30 minutes. Add the mushrooms for the last 15 minutes of cooking. Thicken the sauce with a little of the seasoned flour mixed with a little water.

Makes: 4 servings

62. FRIED RABBIT

From an old cookbook TURKEY DUCK WILD GAME

FRIED RABBIT

Ingredients:

I (21/2-3 lb.) young rabbit out up
I cup milk 1 teaspoon salt
1/4 teaspoon pepper
Flour
1/2 cup butter
1/2 cup shortening
1 cup chicken broth
1/2 cup sour cream (optional)

Preparation:
Dip the pieces of rabbit into the milk and let drain. Lightly season each piece with salt and pepper and drench in the flour.
In a large skillet over medium heat brown the pieces of rabbit on all sides in the butter and or shortening. Lower the heat and cook, covered, until tender, about 45 minutes. Remove rabbit to a hot platter and keep warm. Drain off excess fat keep o tablespoons drippings for the gravy. Make a gravy with pan drippings, using a little flour and chicken broth blend together well, then add sour cream and keep heating but do not boil.

Makes: Four servings.

63. RABBIT STEW

RABBIT STEW

Ingredients:

2 (3 lb.) rabbits cut up
3 teaspoons salt
1/4 teaspoon pepper
1 cup flour
3 slices bacon cut into pieces
3 tablespoons shortening
4 onions sliced
1 clove garlic crushed
3 cups water
1/4 teaspoon marjoram
4 potatoes diced
1 1/2 cups diced carrot
1 teaspoon paprika
1 cup sour cream

Preparation:
In a bowl with the flour seasoned with I teaSpoon salt and 1/4 teaspoon pepper dredge the pieces of rabbit. In a large saucepan over medium heat fry the bacon until crisp. Remove bacon and
drain on paper toweling. Now add the shortening to the bacon drippings in the saucepan and the rabbit pieces until nicely browned. Add the onions, garlic and water. Season with marjoram, 2 teaspoons salt, and 1/4 teaspoon pepper. Cover and simmer until tender. Add the potatoes, carrot, bacon and a little

additional water. Cook until vegetables are tender. Add paprika and sour cream. Reheat but be careful don't let the stew to boil after adding the sour cream it will curdle.

Makes: 8 servings

64. RABBIT FRICASSEE

RABBIT FRICASSEE

Ingredients:

1 (3-4 lb.) rabbit cut up
1/2 cup flour
1 teaspoon salt
1/4 teaspoon pepper
1/4 cup shortening or salad oil
2 cups water
1 tablespoon vinegar
1 onion chopped
1 clove garlic crushed
1/2 bay leaf crushed
1/8 teaspoon thyme
Dumplings, noodles or rice

Preparation:

In a paper or plastic bag mix the flour, salt and pepper. Put the piece of rabbit a few at a time, and shake well.
In a large saucepan over medium heat brown the rabbit in the shortening or oil. When done add water, vinegar, onion, garlic, bay leaf, and thyme. Bring to a boil, cover and simmer until tender, about an hour. Add a little more water if needed. Remove to a warm platter and adjust the seasoning of the gravy. If too thick, thin with a little more water or chicken broth, if too thin, add a bit of the seasoned flour mixed with a little cold water. Pour gravy over

meat and serve with dumplings, noodles or rice. If you decide to serve with dumplings, make them in the fricassee.

Makes: 6 servings

65. Herbs and Garnishings

Herbs and Garnishings appropriate to WILD GAME MEAT

Traditional: Marinade Currant Jelly

Herbs and Spices	Garnishes
Basil	Apples
Bay leaf	Buttermilk
Cloves	Currants
1 Cumin seed	Jelly
Garlic	Lemon
Ginger	Lingon berries
Juniper berries	Orange sauce
Oregano	Pickle relish
Rosemary	Preserves
Sage	Scallions
Savory	Shallots
Thyme	Sour cream
	Vinegar
	Wine

66. Acknowledgements

Thank you for buying this book i hope you will enjoy the many delicious recipes that have been collected for your cooking pleasure.

This book is part of a series for all who are looking for those precious golden recipes that have been guarded closely and handed down over generations. While some of the recipes are a world apart all are in excellent good taste and easy to follow even for first time cook to create. Or maybe you just want to add some delicious dishes to your repertoire you will love this book.

Get All The Books In The Series:
From an Old Cookbook APPLES
From an Old Cookbook FABULOUS FISH
From an Old Cookbook SHELLFISH
From an Old Cookbook SOUPS
From an Old Cookbook CHICKEN

Made in the USA
Monee, IL
25 February 2023